100 Fiverr Orders in 30 days
10 Steps to Career Success with Fiverr

by: Rob Moore

Copyright © 2023 by RobtheMaritimer.com

All rights reserved. This book or any portion thereof may not be reproduced or used in any manner whatsoever without the express written permission of the publisher except for the use of brief quotations in a book review.
First edition, 2021
RobtheMaritimer.com
Ingramport, NS
Canada
Website: RobtheMaritimer.com
Youtube: https://youtube.com/robthemaritimer

Disclaimer: The information contained within this document is for educational purposes only, based solely on our own opinions, and should not be considered professional financial advice. All effort has been executed to present accurate and reliable, complete information. No warranties of any kind are declared or implied.

www.robthemaritimer.com

www.robthemaritimer.com

CONTENTS

Introduction	1
Step 1 - Identify Your Skill(s)	5
Step 2 - Define Your Gig	9
Step 3 - Create a Killer Title	13
Step 4 - Pricing Tips	15
Step 5 - Write Your Description	17
Step 6 - FAQs For Your Gig	19
Step 7 - Gig Video & Thumbnail	21
Step 8 - Complete Your Profile	27
Step 9 - Responding To Messages	29
Step 10 - Reevaluating Your Gigs	31
BONUS - My Killer Pricing Strategy	33
Final Thoughts	37
Resources	39

www.robthemaritimer.com

www.robthemaritimer.com

INTRODUCTION

01

My name is Rob Moore and I've been an "internet entrepreneur" for over 20 years, and a successful Fiverr freelancer for the last 4 years. I decided to write this report to help others achieve success with Fiverr… something I believe to be more than achievable for anyone willing to put in the effort.

This is the second edition of this report, as I've completely updated it for 2023. So if you were wondering if the information in this report still applies today, it absolutely does! It is January 2023 as I write this, and the opportunities available to you in Fiverr have never been better.

Fiverr can be very rewarding and extremely profitable, and although it is relatively easy to set up an account and launch a gig, it can be quite difficult to start getting a steady stream of orders.

That is what I intend to help you with.

In this book, I outline and explain the 10 specific steps that you need to take, if you want to get 100 orders or more, each and every month with Fiverr. I followed these 10 steps when I set up my very first gig, and I continue to follow them whenever I set up a new gig.

But why listen to me? Who am I?

www.robthemaritimer.com

For the last 4 years, I've been a full-time freelancer working exclusively through the Fiverr platform. I do not use any other freelance system and instead focus solely on Fiverr, which provides more than enough work for me. The work I do through Fiverr includes video editing, adding subtitles to videos, creating tutorial videos and recording voiceovers. I've completed over 4,200 jobs (or gigs) and earned over $300,000 US dollars in the last 4 years (a more detailed breakdown can be found later in this book).

This past year I also became a Fiverr Top Rated Seller, and started building a Youtube channel to help teach others how to make a living the way I do, using the Fiverr platform. On my channel, I make videos about freelancing on Fiverr, video editing, youtube, live streaming, and making a living online. If you want to check that out, go to Youtube and search for "Rob the Maritimer".

My intention is not to brag… in fact, there are lots of people earning far more than me through Fiverr. However, if you're having trouble getting Fiverr orders and would like to learn some tips from someone who's had success with the platform, or if you're searching for a way to create your own sustainable, home-based business, then this book will help you.

I believe strongly in the gig economy, and in particular, Fiverr's platform for making it easier for freelancers to find work, and people to find freelancers to work for them. I think we are still in the early stages of the gig economy, and that

www.robthemaritimer.com

more and more people will turn to Fiverr to find freelancers to help them, rather than taking on full-time employees.

I think the prospects for Fiverr as a company are great, as I think there will continue to be a growing need for more and more freelancers on the Fiverr platform.

So without further ado, let's jump right into my 10-step blueprint to career success with Fiverr. These are the steps I took when I created my first gig, and anytime I create new gigs. It will give you the best chance to get 100 Fiverr orders each and every month.

www.robthemaritimer.com

04

www.robthemaritimer.com

STEP 1

IDENTIFY YOUR SKILL(S)

Many of you who are reading this have probably spent considerable time on Youtube searching, "How to make money on Fiverr." Youtube can be a great resource, however, there are a lot of misleading videos out there with titles like, "How to make $1000s on Fiverr with no skills." Although that may seem like a great concept, it is in fact, a lie. Fiverr is not a platform that'll work for you if you have no skills. You need to have some skills. In fact, you need to have a skill that other people don't have or don't have the time to do themselves, in order for those people to want to pay you for that skill.

Category Search
The first thing you need to do is identify the skill (or skills) that you have and can offer for sale on the Fiverr platform. If you're not sure what skill you can offer, a great place to start is to go to the Fiverr home page and browse through their categories to see what other Fiverr sellers are offering. There are hundreds of categories and sub-categories and Fiverr adds new ones all the time. Hover over the "Graphics & Design" category for example, and you'll see over 50 sub-categories for things like Logo Design, Brand Style Guides, Cartoons & Comics, Photoshop Editing, and Resume Design, to name just a few. Other major categories include Digital Marketing, Writing & Translation, Video & Animation, Music & Audio, Programming & Tech, Data, Business and Lifestyle… and most

of those main categories have dozens of sub-categories.

If you're unsure about what skills you have that you can offer through Fiverr, my suggestion is to go through each of these categories and click on the ones that interest you. You'll then be presented with all the gigs being offered within the category you selected. Go through the individual gigs and see what people are offering. Learn what types of services are being offered, and see if there's anything there you think you can do. If you find something, write it down. As you go through all the categories and sub-categories, make a list of all the things you think you can do.

This may seem like a long and tedious process, but it should go fairly quickly… I'm sure there will be lots of categories you don't need to click on simply because they either don't interest you or aren't something you can do anyways… you can just skip those ones.

Search Bar
Another way to search through existing Fiverr gigs is to use the search bar at the top of the Fiverr home page. Simply start typing what you want to search for, and Fiverr will attempt to complete your search term. For example, let's say you want to search for "transcribing videos". If you start typing that in the search bar, by the time you type, "transcr", Fiverr will attempt to complete your search term by listing several options: "transcription", "transcript audio", " transcribe music", "transcribe audio", "spanish transcription", and several others. This is an incredibly powerful tool

because the options Fiverr is presenting you with are the most commonly searched terms containing "transcr". So it's like a validity test. If you see the search term you're looking for "pop up" as a completed search option, you know other people are searching for it as well, and therefore it might be a good option for a gig you can offer for sale.

No Skills?
If you don't have any luck finding suitable gigs using the search options, it might be time to change your way of thinking. Don't make the mistake of thinking you have to be an expert in your field in order to sell through Fiverr. You don't. You only have to be better than the person that needs the skill. You may not be able to charge as much as someone who is an expert, but there could very well still be a market for someone with average skills.

Another thing I like to suggest is to keep an eye out for gigs that you think you'd like to learn how to do, but perhaps don't feel comfortable doing yet. This could be a great opportunity to learn a new skill. Fiverr has a lot of online courses covering a lot of the skills offered through Fiverr gigs through their "Learn from Fiverr" site. In addition, you could also learn new skills through udemy.com, and of course, Youtube.

Once you've identified a skill to target, it's time to define your first gig.

08

www.robthemaritimer.com

STEP 2

DEFINE YOUR GIG

When creating a new gig, the first thing you should do is go back to Fiverr and search for similar gigs offered by other sellers. Search for the same service you want to offer, and then analyze the gigs that come up. There may be thousands of similar gigs, so you'll want to be selective in the gigs you analyze. Don't click on any yet, just browse over the gigs in the search results and look for the following:

Star Rating
Only look at gigs that have 5-star ratings. If there aren't any, then look at 4.9-star ratings. You want to model your gig after only the most successful gigs.

Number of Reviews
Next to the star rating is the number of reviews that gig has received. The higher the number, the more successful the gig.

Seller Level
Under the seller's username will be their Seller Level. You'll see either Level 1, Level 2, Top Rated Seller, or there won't be anything. You'll want to concentrate on gigs where the seller is either Level 2 or Top Rated, as they are the most successful sellers. There may be some good gigs by Level 1 sellers, but keep in mind that to reach level 1, you only need to be an active seller for 60 days, earn $400, maintain a

www.robthemaritimer.com

4.7-star rating (and a few other things), whereas Level 2 or higher requires earning $2,000 and being an active seller for at least 120 days, so that's where you'll find the more successful sellers.

Price
Don't pay too much attention to the price, since the price listed here is the minimum starting price. But in looking at the most successful sellers (highest rated, most reviews), take note of what their minimum price is.

Fiver's Choice
If you see a gig that has the "Fiver's Choice" badge in the description, this is one you want to include in your research because they are gigs that have had a lot of positive ratings, so much so that the team at Fiverr is recommending them.

The gigs you've identified here are your competition. They are the gigs you'll want to be better than when creating your own gig, so keep that in mind.

Now that you've identified some gigs to analyze, you'll want to get yourself a pen and paper, or what I typically do is start a new Google Sheets spreadsheet. For each gig you've identified, write down their title, the seller's level, their average rating, and number of reviews.

Next, you'll want to click on each of these gigs for further analysis. You'll be taken to the gig details page. One of the most important indicators of whether or not a gig is performing well is the number of "Orders in Queue", and this number will be displayed to the right of their total number of ratings if they have any. So look for the "Orders in Queue" and make a note of how many they have, if any.

Look at their offer details on the right-hand side. Write down their starting price, what they offer for that price, and what other pricing levels they offer. Also, make a note of their delivery time.

I like to look at the number of orders in queue in conjunction with their shortest delivery time. If they have a lot of orders in queue, and their delivery time is short (say 24 hours), then that indicates that the gig gets a lot of daily orders.

You should also scroll down to read their gig description, and take note of whether or not they've created a gig video. Having a gig video is one of the things I think is imperative to having a successful gig, but not every gig has one.

Once you've written down all the above information for the gigs you'll be competing with, choose some of the better ones, and use those gigs as templates from which you'll make your own gig. Remember, you're not recreating the wheel here, someone is probably already offering exactly what you want to offer, and that's ok. Competition is good, and no one has the capacity to deliver on all orders that will be coming into Fiverr. So even if you offer the exact same thing as 100 other sellers, if there are thousands of people looking for the service, there'll be more than enough work to be spread

www.robthemaritimer.com

around all the gigs that offer that service.

To give yourself the best chance at getting noticed, however, try to think of ways you can beat the other gig offers or other things you can add to help differentiate yourself.

STEP 3

CREATE A KILLER TITLE

Now that you've got a good idea of what you want to offer, it's time to create your gig title. Your gig title is one of the most important parts of your gig, for two reasons. First, along with your gig thumbnail, your title is what's displayed first when people are searching for a gig to purchase. Therefore, your title should clearly state what your gig offers. Secondly, since the words in your gig title effectively become keywords that purchasers are searching for, you'll want to include keywords in your title for which you want your gig to show up in the search.

What I suggest you should do first, is make a list of the keywords you want to target with your gig... words or terms that you think people will type into the search bar when looking for your specific gig. Once you have this list, type them into the search bar and make sure your competitor's gigs show up in the results. You can also check the number of results returned in the search, and if there are more than a couple thousand, consider getting more specific with your keyword search. For example, the search term "transcribe video" returns 5,803 results, but if we get more specific and search for "transcribe documentary video", that returns only 369 results. So try to be as specific as you can when targeting keyword phrases, and then make sure to include those keyword phrases in your title, as well as your description.

Once you have identified the keyword phrase you want to target, use it to create a title for your gig that is clear, to the

www.robthemaritimer.com

point, and written in proper English. Don't just randomly throw words together... they should make sense and be easy to understand. If English is not your first language, then you should have someone who is fluent in English check your title to make sure it makes sense (the same goes for your description, but we'll get to that later).

Using the example keyword phrase above, "transcribe documentary video", you could create any of the following titles:

"I will transcribe your documentary video"
"I will transcribe your documentary video in 24 hours"
"I will do documentary video transcribing"
"I will transcribe your English documentary video"

These are all good examples of ways you could incorporate your keyword phrase into your title and if you've chosen proper keywords that your main competition is using successfully, this should work well for you.

www.robthemaritimer.com

STEP 4

PRICING TIPS

The next step is to set your pricing. You probably already have a good idea of what you can price your services for, so you now just have to define it. With Fiverr, you have the choice of setting up 1 price for your service, or you can offer 3 different "packages" or pricing tiers. Choose the option that works best for you, but I would gravitate toward the packages option, as long as your service can be defined and priced that way.

When deciding how to set your prices, take a look at how your competition structured their prices, and what they offer. Pay particular attention to the competition gigs that are the most successful, and see what they are charging and how long their delivery times are. The most successful gigs in your niche can be used as a gauge that shows how much you can charge in the future, once your gig is established. I don't recommend pricing your services as high as the most successful gigs, at least not when you're just starting out with a new gig. Instead, price your gig lower than theirs, at least until you have a good number of orders coming in.

Price your services as low as you can, AND set your delivery as short as you possibly can. Why? When you're first starting out, the goal should not be to make a huge profit right away. Instead, you should aim to get as many orders as you can, do as good a job for your clients as you can, and deliver them as fast as you can. The goal here is to start building your portfolio and start collecting 5-star ratings from super happy clients. Don't

www.robthemaritimer.com

worry about earnings and profit just yet… they'll come later.

When pricing Fiverr gigs you have to be super specific about what you're offering and at what price. It is no good to simply say, "I will transcribe your video for $5". What if the client sends you a video that's 2 hours long, which would take you many hours to transcribe? Should you charge the same for that as you would for a 2-minute video? Probably not. So when designing your pricing strategy, make sure to define the parameters around how much work you'll offer for your set price. Using our transcribing example again, you could charge $5 to transcribe a video that's up to 5 minutes long. And an example of how you could use the pricing packages option is you could set up 3 tiers of pricing for three different video lengths, like $5 for 5-minute videos, $10 for 10-minute videos, and $20 for videos up to 20 minutes… something like that.

You also have to be specific about the delivery time. The Fiverr system allows you to set the number of days for delivery for each price level you set up. When setting your delivery times, set them as low as you reasonably can, making sure you can complete the service within the time frame you set. It is going to be critically important that you always deliver jobs before their due date, as that will help your gig rank higher in search results.

STEP 5

WRITE YOUR DESCRIPTION

The gig description is where you'll describe the details of what you are offering. You have a limit of 1,200 characters to use, and you also have the ability to use bold, highlighting, bullet points, and numbered lists. Spend some time to make sure your description is clear, well-written with proper English grammar, and pleasing to the eye. Use bold and highlights sparingly, and only to point out important things that you don't want your readers to miss. If you use them too often, it'll defeat the purpose of using them at all. You should take some time looking at other gig's descriptions, particularly descriptions for successful gigs. Also, make sure that you've covered everything you should, and a good way to check this is to look at the gig descriptions of your successful competitor gigs and see what they've included in their descriptions. This may give you some good ideas on what to include in your own description.

If you have too much information to fit within the 1,200-character limit but you feel it all must be included, then use the FAQ section for some of your description points so you can remove them from your description. For example, you may have planned on including the following in your description, "I can also transcribe French videos as well, so if you have a French video you want to be transcribed, be sure to message me and ask for a quote." You could remove that entire section from your description to save on your character limit, and instead create a FAQ with the question, "Do you transcribe videos in languages other than English?" And then put the answer, "Yes, I also transcribe French videos. Please message me for details, and send me your video so I can have a look!"

The last point I'll make about the description is that you want to make sure to include your target keyword phrase in your description, but make sure everything is still grammatically correct and doesn't sound like you're simply stuffing keywords into your description. Including your target keyword phrase in your description as well as your title will really help in ranking your gig higher in Fiverr's search algorithm.

STEP 6

FAQS FOR YOUR GIG

The next step in creating your gig is filling out the FAQ section. There are a lot of gigs that don't even bother to include this section as it is optional. However, if you want to give yourself the best chance of success, I highly recommend including at least a few questions and answers here, even if you think they are basic and self-explanatory. You want to come across to your potential clients as someone who is going above and beyond to provide help, and answering some basic questions in the FAQ before they are even asked is a great way to do that.

Another advantage of the FAQ section is if you are struggling to fit all of what you want to say in your description, as I mentioned in the previous section. That is, if you've reached the 1,200 character limit in your description but still have more you need to say to properly describe your gig, you can remove some things from your description and instead include them as questions and answers in your FAQ. Think of it as an extension of your description.

Include at least three questions and answers in your FAQ, and when finished, move on to the next step.

www.robthemaritimer.com

20

www.robthemaritimer.com

STEP 7

GIG VIDEO & THUMBNAIL

You can set up your gig without a gig video, but I highly recommend against that. Having a gig video is super important when it comes to getting clicks on your gig when someone does a gig search, mainly because people are just more apt to want to watch a video than look at an image. So much more information can be conveyed in a video than an image, and so if someone is wanting to learn more about what you're offering, they'll be more likely to click on your gig if they see you have a gig video.

When gigs are shown on a search results page, you can tell which ones have gig videos and which ones don't, as the ones with gig videos have a small play button in the upper right corner. A good exercise to do is to go to Fiverr and search for any gig. On the results page, look at how many gigs have gig videos and how many don't. What you'll probably find is that the majority of gigs do not have gig videos… and I think that's a huge opportunity wasted by those sellers.

Now let's talk about how to create your gig video. I could teach an entire course on creating gig videos as there are so many different ways to create them and so many different types of videos you can create… but instead of going through all that, let me try to break it down into your basic options for creating videos.

www.robthemaritimer.com

Types of gig videos

Cartoon Explainer videos - Colorful, fun videos that deliver your message in a creative way. Usually contains voiceover and background music.

Still Image videos - Can have 1 image throughout the entire video (perhaps a thumbnail you create), and includes voiceover and sometimes music. These are good for voiceover-type gigs where you want to showcase your voice.

Slide Presentation videos - These are like Powerpoint presentations converted into videos. They can have nice transitions between slides, and often have voiceover and/or music.

Demo style videos - Simply refers to a video that showcases your work. Voiceover artists will want to showcase their voice, logo designers may want to showcase their designs, and video creators will want to showcase their video productions.

"Meet the Seller" videos - This is when the seller (that's you) appears in the video to deliver their message themselves.

Voiceover or Subtitles?

Should you use voiceover or subtitles in your videos? Or both? I strongly recommend using voiceover as that's the clearest way to deliver your message. You can also add music to the background, and you can add subtitles as well. But in my experience, a video with a nice clear voiceover will be

www.robthemaritimer.com

much more professional and will make it easier for the seller to learn what you are providing in your gig.

Your voice vs AI voice vs hiring a voiceover talent?
I am a big believer in using your own voice if possible because people love getting to know who they'll be working with. It also projects authenticity which people also love. But if that's not possible, perhaps if you don't have the proper equipment to record yourself, then hiring a voiceover talent is a good alternative. I strongly recommend against using an AI voice, as they do not sound well and will just make your video sound like an amateur made it. If you're trying to decide between using your own voice or hiring a voiceover talent, just remember that even if you don't think you sound as good as a professional voiceover artist, that doesn't matter (unless your gig is for selling voiceover work!)... the authenticity of you, the seller, using your own voice in your video will win you more points with buyers than a professionally trained voiceover artist delivering your message for you.

Show yourself, or not?
If at all possible, show yourself. Be the star of your own video! Again, just as with using your own voice, if you, the seller, put yourself in front of the camera to deliver your message yourself, that is the absolute best way to project authenticity to your buyers, and also helps them to get to know you and your personality. People underestimate how important that is! If I were to pick one thing that I did when setting up my first gig that had the most impact on the success of my gig, it was me making my own video. All I did

www.robthemaritimer.com

was I wrote a short script, held my iPhone up at arm's length away, and recorded myself delivering my message. I only spoke for about 20 seconds, then I used video editing software to add some samples of my work to fill up the rest of the 75-second video. Did that video look professional? Not at all! In fact, I look back on that video and can't believe the success I've had with that gig, considering how unprofessional that video looks! You can check it out if you visit my profile at www.fiverr.com/themaritimer, and click the "Add professional synced subtitles to your video" gig. In case I upgrade that gig video, you can always find the original on my youtube channel at www.youtube.com/robthemaritimer, click "Videos" and then scroll to the bottom... the first video I ever posted to the channel. That's my best-selling gig and it accounts for probably 75% of my Fiverr business.

Do it yourself or hire someone?
This will depend on your budget and your comfort level with the software you'll need to use. Creating a video at the very least requires video editing software, and there are inexpensive ones available that you can use. I personally use Camtasia Studio as I find it easy to use and I've been using it for many years. Other video editing software options include Davinci Resolve (I'm using this more and more), Adobe Premiere Pro, Final Cut Pro, and Filmora... and you can also find some free options as well.

If you are looking to create cartoon-style explainer videos, then you could look at online software like Vyond (formerly

www.robthemaritimer.com

GoAnimate), Doodly, Animaker, Explaindio, or VideoMakerFX.

If you don't feel like you have the skills to put together a video, then there are a ton of Fiverr sellers who can help out with any of the above types of videos.

My recommendation
I strongly recommend putting yourself in your videos. This doesn't mean you have to create the final video yourself because you could hire a video editor to do that. If you make any mistakes while recording yourself, don't worry, because a good video editor can edit those mistakes out.

Gig Thumbnail
The thumbnail is the image that shows up for your gig when people find your gig on Fiverr. If you don't have a gig video and only have images for your gig, then one of those images can be set as your thumbnail. If you do have a gig video, then your thumbnail will have to be a screenshot that comes from within your gig video. Luckily, you can set which part of your video is to be your thumbnail. To do this, once your gig video has been uploaded and approved, you'll be able to edit the thumbnail and choose any location within your video to set as your thumbnail. Since you have this flexibility, I strongly recommend designing a thumbnail for your video as an image and then importing that image into your video during the editing process. Set it to display for 1 second either at the very beginning of your video, or the very end and then once it's part of your gig video you'll be able to select it as your thumbnail after your video is uploaded. When designing your

www.robthemaritimer.com

thumbnail, you can use software like Photoshop or online software like Canva, or if you don't feel you have the skills to make a good one, you can hire a designer on Fiverr to make your thumbnail for you. One final thought on your gig video thumbnail is that it should be designed to support your gig title. Remember the target keyword phrase you chose for your gig and included in your title and description? You should include that as text in your gig thumbnail as well, along with any other supporting information you want.

STEP 8

COMPLETE YOUR PROFILE

By now you probably already have your profile setup, as you would've set that up when you created your Fiverr account and you would've had to do that in order to create your gig... however, what you should do at this point is revisit your Fiverr profile to make sure it is complete. From the Fiverr home page, click your account icon in the top right and that will take you to your profile page. Make sure you have a good image of yourself in your profile image. I strongly recommend a real photo of yourself and not a cartoon version or a logo, because remember that you'll be selling yourself as much as you're selling your gig. People want to buy from people they can relate to. I view the profile image as the most important part of anyone's profile on Fiverr.

Below your username, there is a small area where you can insert a tagline. Be sure to fill that out... I simply put in, "Let's work together!"

Next is the description, in my view the second most important part of your profile next to your profile image. Write a compelling description of yourself, describe who you are and what your skills are. The description is another opportunity to sell yourself, and to convince potential buyers that you are indeed someone they will want to work with.

www.robthemaritimer.com

Continue completing your profile by selecting the languages you speak, and linking other social media accounts to your account. The skills section is where you can add all the skills you think potential buyers might be interested in. And finally, complete the education section at the bottom by listing the schools you've attended, degrees you obtained, etc.

The bottom line with your profile is that a lot of people who are looking to buy a gig will quite often click on a seller's username to go to their profile and learn more about them. With that in mind, it's a really good idea to complete your profile section as thoroughly as you can.

STEP 9

RESPONDING TO MESSAGES

With your gig all set up and your profile updated, you're all ready to start receiving orders! However, a lot of potential buyers will message a seller with questions before they purchase a gig. If you do receive a message, it is imperative that you answer as soon as you possibly can... especially when you're a new seller. One of the metrics Fiverr uses in deciding which gigs to show at the top of search results is "average response time". You'll see this metric on anyone's profile page. The lower your average response time, the better your gigs will rank in search results... and the lowest average response time that Fiverr will show is 1 hour. You want to try as best as you can to keep your average response time at that 1-hour level.

Do I have to answer messages in the middle of the night?
Well, yes and no. If you receive the majority of your messages during the day and you're able to respond immediately, then that will give you some leeway when you can't respond right away in the middle of the night. So for example, if you get 5 messages during the day that you were able to answer within 5 minutes, and then got 2 messages overnight that you didn't respond to until the next morning (say 4 hours and 2 hours later), then your average response rate will be:

Minutes to respond to 7 messages:
[5 + 5 + 5 + 5 + 5 + 240 + 120] = 385 minutes, or an average of 385 / 7 = 55 minutes.

The above example will result in your average response rate being set at 1 hour, the lowest possible score that Fiverr will show… and that would be great!

Fiverr Mobile App
When I first started with Fiverr, one of the things I did right away is I downloaded the Fiverr iOS app to my iPhone. This is a great tool and will allow you to respond to messages from the app, so you don't always have to be in your office to respond. Make sure you download that app… there's an Android version as well.

Another thing to keep in mind is that Fiverr only counts your "first responses" in their average response time calculation. So if you respond to someone's first message to you within 5 minutes, but then they respond to your message and you then take 3 hours to respond again, that response is not counted. So just make sure to always respond as quickly as you possibly can to someone's first message to you, and try to keep your average response time at the lowest level of 1 hour. Not only does this help you in Fiverr's search algorithm, but it also is a great indicator to potential buyers that you are someone who responds quickly to messages.

STEP 10

REEVALUATING YOUR GIGS

The final step in my 10-step blueprint to career success with Fiverr is simply to periodically reevaluate your gigs. Once you have everything set up the way you want, give it a couple of weeks and see how things go. Are you getting messages? Are you getting orders? Based on the number of messages and orders you're getting, is there anything you can do to improve your gig's performance? After some time, go back and revisit your competition's gigs. Are their prices still the same? Are they still getting the same number of orders? Have they changed their descriptions or gig videos? After some time passes, have a look at your own gig video and see if you can improve it. Perhaps you went with a cartoon-style explainer video to start, but you find you aren't getting the number of orders you feel you should be. If so, perhaps take some time to consider redoing your video and putting yourself in it. If this makes you uncomfortable or you don't think you're able to do that, maybe study up on some techniques that will help you learn how to be better on camera. There are a ton of things that go into making good videos, and if you start down that rabbit hole you'll probably never stop learning new things… but you will improve. One idea I like to suggest for people who aren't confident in making a full 60 or 75-second video of themselves, is just to do a 20-second intro of yourself, and replace only the first 20 seconds of your video with the video of you. You basically only have to introduce

www.robthemaritimer.com

yourself, tell people what you offer, and tell people to watch the following samples of your work. That's it! Just make sure you're smiling, you're in a well-lit area, and just try to have fun with it. People will love the authenticity and you'll be surprised at how much that will help your gig performance.

The main point of this 10th step is that you should periodically revisit your gigs and always look for ways to improve them. Gigs will stagnate over time, new sellers will enter your market and some old sellers will leave. The gigs that were the top gigs in your category will likely change over time as well, so it's always good to stay on top of the gigs in your niche, know what they're charging, know what delivery times they're offering, and just know who your competition is. That will put you in a much better position to know what to do with your own gig to continue to improve your gig's performance.

www.robthemaritimer.com

BONUS STEP

MY KILLER PRICING STRATEGY

I just want to talk a little about what I think your overall pricing strategy should be, and to walk through what I did when I started and the changes I've made along the way as my Fiverr business was growing.

When you're starting out, you need to be able to differentiate yourself from your competition. For example, if none of your competitors have a gig video that explains what they offer, then you could have a gig video and that alone will differentiate you from them. Another example would be if all your competitors are offering 5-day deliveries or longer… you could then offer a 3-day delivery and be the fastest to deliver in your niche (just be sure the 3-day delivery is achievable… you never want to be late). But sometimes it can be difficult to find something that will differentiate you from your competition, and in this case what I recommend in the beginning is to price your gig as low as you possibly can, and set your delivery time as low as you possibly can as well. Even if you aren't going to generate a profit and could possibly even lose money on an order, what your focus needs to be in the very beginning is to simply get orders into your gig. You absolutely need orders so that you can deliver a great job and then get 5-star ratings, to kickstart the growth of your gig. Your mindset should be that you're investing your time and a possible small loss in profit during your first month until orders start rolling in.

Once orders finally do start coming in, your gig will start ranking higher, and will get more and more impressions when people search for your service. That will result in more people messaging you, and more orders coming in. At this point, you should resist the urge to raise your prices, because you don't want to stop the momentum. If you do become too busy, then the first thing you should do is make your delivery time longer, but keep your price the same. If you continue to get even busier, then make your delivery time longer again, and at this point, you can offer gig extras for faster deliveries, which could increase your profits as well. But whenever you make changes like this, you have to monitor your gig's progress and make a note of any changes. By increasing your standard delivery times, did that result in fewer orders? Did you start getting "rush" orders for which people were paying extra for faster deliveries? How was your overall profit affected? These are all questions you should be able to answer, so be sure to track your progress so you can see what results from the changes that you make.

When I first started with my "video subtitling" gig, I offered to "transcribe and subtitle videos of up to 10 minutes for $5 within 24 hours". That's a lot of work for $5... actually, $4 since Fiverr takes their 20% or $1 cut! But what it did is it jump-started my gig and got some orders rolling in. Once I became busy with that, I changed the 24-hour delivery to a 3-day delivery, but offered a 24-hour rush option for an extra $20. A surprising number of people paid the extra $20 for the rush service. As I continued to get busier, I increased my standard delivery to 5 days, but offered 2 rush options... $20 for 24 hours, or $40 for "right away, but message me first!" I needed people to message me first because what if they sent in an order right after I went to bed? So if they message me first, I'd be able to tell them how quickly I could deliver.

With this strategy, what starts out as a $5 gig can very easily turn into a $45 order if they want delivery within say 1 or 2 hours.

With this pricing strategy in place, I found a lot of people started requesting the subtitling of much longer videos. I soon found out that $5 to transcribe and subtitle up to 10 minutes of video was not sustainable (which I knew anyways... remember, I only priced it that way in the beginning to jump-start the orders coming in). So the next thing I did was change my gig to be $5 to transcribe and subtitle videos up to 5 minutes. Then the next thing I did was I separated the transcribing from the subtitling, and I offered to subtitle videos only and required my clients to provide me with a transcript. If they didn't have a transcript, then I could offer to transcribe the video as well, for an extra charge.

So my point in all this is, if you can start off by charging a really low amount for your gig so that you can kick start its growth, there will be opportunities to raise your prices later on, and different pricing strategies you can implement so that the pricing increases don't scare off all your clients. Just make sure to always monitor how your gig is performing, so

www.robthemaritimer.com

36

that you can always backtrack if you make a change that doesn't work out well.

FINAL THOUGHTS

I obviously can't guarantee that following the above steps will guarantee you 100 orders per month. However, it did work for me, and doing so will give you the best chance for success.

How many orders did I get when I first started selling through Fiverr? My very first month I got 2 orders, and earned $44. I got zero orders in my second month, and then I got 5 orders in my third month after I created my gig video. My fourth month saw 5 new orders totaling $31, and then in my 5th month, I got 38 new orders and made over $700. The next month I got over 100 orders and made over $3,000 and I went on to earn $49,192 in my first full year as a Fiverr seller, and I averaged over 100 orders per month during that year (1,431 orders in 2019 to be exact). And if you do the math, that works out to an average of $34.37 per order, even though the gig was listed at "starting at $5".

So this system has worked for me and is still working for me three years later. I don't get as many orders as I used to, but that's because I now charge more for my services and I'm earning more per order. My average order size is consistently over $100 every month and I've had some orders as large as several thousand dollars for some very large jobs. But my best-selling gig, the gig that brings in most of my business, is still the same "I will add subtitles to your video" gig and my starting price is now at $10.

www.robthemaritimer.com

If you have a skill or a service that businesses need, then Fiverr is a fantastic way to earn a very healthy living in today's gig economy.

Good luck to you, and feel free to contact me if you have any questions. The best way to reach me is by visiting my Youtube channel and messaging me through the comments section of any of my videos. Or you can visit my Fiverr account and message me there. I'll be setting up more ways to get in touch with me, but for now, Youtube is probably the best way.

All the best!

Rob Moore

Website: RobtheMaritimer.com
Youtube: https://youtube.com/robthemaritimer
Instagram: https://instagram.com/rob_themaritimer
Fiverr: https://fiverr.com/themaritimer

RESOURCES

Fiverr (www.fiverr.com) - the best freelancer platform connecting millions of buyers with sellers.

Youtube (www.youtube.com) - My #1 resource for learning how to do things I don't know how to do.

Trello (www.trello.com) - a great resource for managing your business.

Google Sheets (www.google.com) - I use it every day to track my daily and monthly Fiverr orders.

Camtasia Studio (www.techsmith.com/camtasia) - The video editing software I use to edit videos, add subtitles, and do screen recordings.

Canva (www.canva.com) - Easy-to-use online software for creating thumbnails and other images.

Adobe Audition (www.adobe.com) - The software I use to record and edit my voiceovers.

www.robthemaritimer.com

Made in the USA
Middletown, DE
19 January 2023